ISBN 978-1-998317-67-7

Cover design by Charlotte Chang.

First Edition: January, 2025

Giraffe

Raccoon

Squirrel

Wild Boar

Horse

Camel

Beaver

Brown Bear

Goat

Polar Bear

Alpaca

Arctic Fox

Swan

Cat

Ermine

Rabbit

Gazelle

Lion

Golden Monkey

Kangaroo

Golden retriever dog

Yellow oriole

Fennec Fox

Dingo

Canary

Sulphur butterfly

Crow

Panther

Black Bear

Chimpanzee

Silver Fox

Tasmanian Devil

Gibbon

Black Drongo

Red Panda

Red Fox

Red Kangaroo

Orangutan

Flamingo

Scarlet Macaw

Mandrill

Vermilion Flycatcher

Praying Mantis

Emerald dove

Parakeet

Green barbet

Zebra

Skunk

Penguin

Panda

Badger

Snowy Owl

Malayan Tapir

Ring~Tailed Lemur

Leopard

Okapi

Spotted Hyena

Ocelot

Appaloosa horse

African Wild Dog

Spotted deer

Tiger

Kingfisher

Peacock

Blue Jay

Blue Morpho Butterfly

Hyacinth macaw

Blue Poison Dart Frog

Indigo bunting

Bluebird

Otter

Rhinoceros

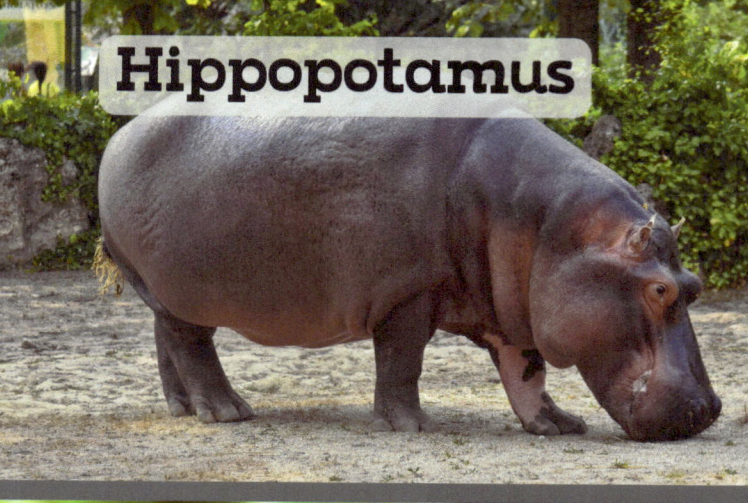

Hippopotamus

Mole

Elephant

Wombat

Gray Wolf

Donkey

Chinchilla

Parrot

Mandarin Duck

Toucan

Rainbow Lorikeet

Monarch Butterfly

Golden Pheasant

Harlequin Tree Frog

Golden Lion Tamarin

Ladybug

Quetzal

Hamster

Capybara

Hedgehog

Meerkat

Sloth

Agouti

Bison